WORLD WINDOWS
In the
Neighborhood

HEINLE
CENGAGE Learning™

Y|S|G
A YBM COMPANY
Young & Son
Global, Inc.

What places are in your neighborhood?

Contents

Vocabulary

post office

bank

bakery

4

school

restaurant

hospital

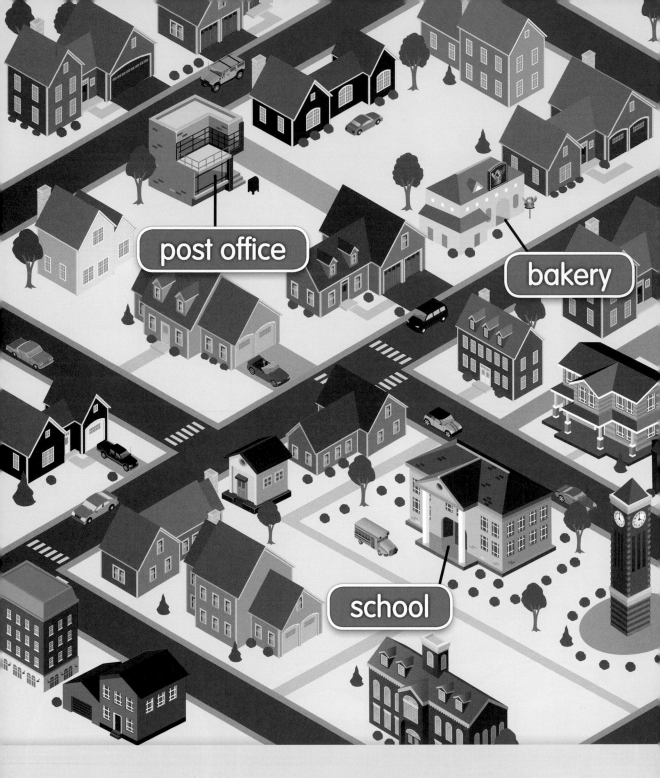

post office

bakery

school

This is a neighborhood.

A neighborhood has many places for people to go.

Here is the post office.
People send letters at the post office.

Here is the bank.

People keep money at the bank.

Here is the bakery.

People buy bread at the bakery.

Here is the school.
People learn things at school.

Here is the restaurant.

People eat at the restaurant.

Here is the hospital.

Sick people go to the hospital.

13

What places can you find in a neighborhood?

In Your Neighborhood

Do you go to the bakery,
The restaurant, the post office?
Do you go to the hospital
That's in your neighborhood?

Do you go to the bakery,
The restaurant, the post office?
Do you go to the hospital
That's in your neighborhood?

15

Index